11/13

Math on the Job

Math at the Hospital

Tracey Steffora

Chicago, Illinois

Edited by Dan Nunn and Abby Colich
Designed by Victoria Allen
Picture research by Tracy Cummins
Production control by Vicki Fitzgerald

Printed and bound in China by Leo Paper Group

15 14 13 12
10 9 8 7 6 5 4 3 2 1

Library of Congress Cataloging-in-Publication Data
Steffora, Tracey.
   Math at the hospital / Tracey Steffora.
      p. cm.—(Math on the job)
   Includes index.
   ISBN 978-1-4329-7152-6 (hb)—ISBN 978-1-4329-7159-5 (pb)
   1. Hospitals—Juvenile literature. 2. Mathematics—Juvenile literature. I. Title.

   RA963.5.S738 2013
   362.1101′51—dc23

   2012013371

Acknowledgments
The author and publishers are grateful to the following for permission to reproduce copyright material: Corbis: p. 8 (© Kai Chiang/Golden Pixels LLC); dreamstime: p. 12 (Indianeye); Getty Images: pp. 11 (© Claver Carroll), 14 (Blend Images/ERproductions Ltd), 15 (ZEPHYR), 19 (Sean Locke), 20 (LWA); iStockphoto: pp. 5 (© Christopher Futcher); Shutterstock: pp. 4 (Stephen Coburn), 6 (wavebreakmedia ltd), 7 (Marlon Lopez), 9 (Tubol Evgeniya), 10 (Alexander Raths), 13 (michaeljung), 16 (Dario Sabljak), 17 (momopixs), 18 (Alexander Raths), 21 (vgstudio), 21 clock (erashov), 22a (Alexander Raths), 22b (Alexander Raths).

Front cover photograph of a doctor taking a patient's temperature reproduced with permission from Jose Luis Pelaez Inc.

Back cover photograph of nurse and patient looking at thermometer at hospital reproduced with permission from Shutterstock (wavebreakmedia ltd).

Every effort has been made to contact copyright holders of any material reproduced in this book. Any omissions will be rectified in subsequent printings if notice is given to the publisher.

Contents

Math at the Hospital

Many people work at the hospital.

Many people use math at
the hospital.

Measuring

thermometer

The nurse measures how warm.

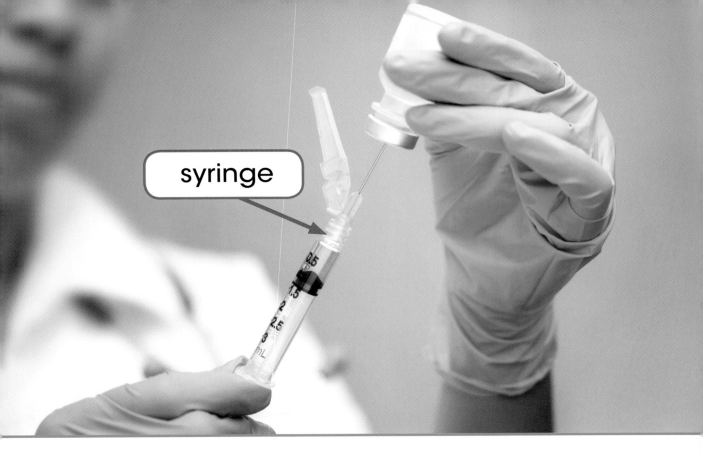

syringe

The nurse measures how much.

scale

The nurse measures how heavy.

baby

girl

Who is heavier? The baby or
the girl? (answer on page 22)

Counting

The doctor counts heartbeats.

The doctor counts fingers.

The doctor counts toes.

How many toes can you count?

(answer on page 22)

Shapes

x-ray

The doctor looks at bones.

These bones are straight.

This bone is curved.

Is this bone straight or curved?

(answer on page 22)

Time

The nurse knows what time to give medicine.

patient

The nurse knows what time to feed patients.

The doctor knows what time to see patients.

What time does the doctor see this patient? (answer on page 22)

Answers

page 9:   The girl is heavier than the baby.

page 13:   There are ten toes.

page 17:   The bone is curved.

page 21:   The doctor sees the patient at 2:00.

Picture Glossary

heartbeat sound that happens when the heart pumps blood

medicine something given to treat illness

Index

Notes for parents and teachers
Math is a way that we make sense of the world around us. For the young child, this includes recognizing similarities and differences, classifying objects, recognizing shapes and patterns, developing number sense, and using simple measurement skills.

Before reading
Connect with what children know.
Discuss that a hospital is a place where people go when they are sick or hurt. Talk about the many jobs that people do in a hospital that care for people, and encourage children to share any experiences they have had being taken care of by a doctor or nurse.

After reading
Build upon children's curiosity and desire to explore.
Identify some of the different tools that are used by doctors and nurses, such as a scale, stethoscope, thermometer—as well as some of the machines, such as an x-ray machine and an echocardiogram machine.

If possible, have a stethoscope available and help children to hear and count their heart as it beats.